Evincepub
Publishing

Evincepub Publishing

Parijat Extension, Bilaspur, Chhattisgarh 495001
First Published by Evincepub Publishing 2021

ISBN: 978-93-5446-018-0

Tryst With Pandemic

"IN THE MEMORY OF THOSE BRAVE HEARTS THAT STOPPED BEATING DUE TO COVID-19"

When the whole world is appreciating the efforts taken by the corona warriors to ensure everyone's safety everywhere, we are no exceptions, "We salute the brave Corona warriors for their tireless effort to deliver essential services." This pandemic poses a greater threat to mankind, and at this point of time we should keep our differences apart and join hands to save the one planet we got. We extend our heartfelt condolences to the bereaved families of those who lost their lives. The Pandemic though caused valuable lives but even exposed us to new learning curves with all its facets. Along with the social distancing came the bridging of family bonding which was distanced over the times. The healthy measures that were overlooked also implemented without leaving much choice.

The Swach Bharat Abhiyan – which was an attempt to bring hygiene among communities – was made more objective with the nature's vehement directions. Nature which is the creator's manifestation of beauty is not only beautiful but also is a teacher to mankind. It appears as the Creator's way of teaching mankind the callous behavior of human beings towards nature. It was a cleansing process through non-violence where one could observe the compassion of human beings towards animals. People made it a point to feed the stray animals who would otherwise be starving and killed. The homeless were given shelter and the distance between the haves and have not's was bridged. The ethos that was shared by people towards their fellow beings was something each one of us looks forward to. With the busy schedules, people had forgotten to be empathetic. The period of lockdown naturally taught to stand in solidarity with fellow human beings.

Nothing comes easy and so the lessons learned were also after the sacrifice of individuals who are rightly termed as "Warriors" who through their sacrifice taught life's greatest lessons that money can buy all but not happiness and life. The power of materialism, which has blindfolded all, was made to realize all that works is love, compassion and humanity. Hence rightly goes the saying service to humanity is service to God.

ACKNOWLEDGEMENT

As we come towards the final step, our efforts could not be given a shape without the blessings and best wishes of numerous people who helped us in our endeavor. We express our gratitude to all of them for helping us at various stages.

Everything is destined we are just a medium to execute it. We bow to The Almighty for choosing us for this cause.

Firstly, we would like to thank our families and well-wishers for their valuable support, without whom the journey wouldn't be possible. We are indebted to our Gurus for grooming us and giving us an opportunity to call us their disciple.

Our sincere thanks to our respective Institutions for their encouragement and guidance – Siksha 'O' Anusandhan (Deemed to be university) and SRM Institute of Science and Technology. We also thank Our Chancellors, Vice Chancellors and all the faculty members.

We express our sincere gratitude to Sri Manoj Nayak, The President of Siksha 'O' Anusandhan and Dr. R Shivakumar, Chairman SRM Group of Institutions Ramapuram and Trichy Campuses.

We are lucky as we are blessed with one of the greatest academicians and Administrators Dr. V Subbiah Bharathi, who with his moving words carved a beautiful message for all of us.

We are thankful to Dr. Tirtha Prasad Mukhopadhay, a living legend for his mentorship and inputs. We are equally thankful to Prof. Tarun Tapas Mukherjee for his support and contribution. Our special thanks to Mr. Harsh Vardhan Bhanot, Joint Secretary, Ministry of Finance, Govt. of India for his wishes and encouragement.

Our sincere thanks to Evincepub Publishing house and all the members associated. But on a very personal note thanks to Vikas Singh Thakur for his suggestions and cooperation.

We thank Swayam Prabha Foundation, Jarnsdel Bharathi Institute for Policy and Global Reforms, Centre for Statistics and Analysis for their help to carry out the research and survey. We thank all the members of Centre for Statistics and Analysis, because of you all we got unhampered survey report in the exact way we wanted.

Sincerely, we thank the team at the backend, Rahul, Souradipta, Debolina, Prashanth, Shayeri, Tithi, Dristi, Siddhartha, Aarti for helping us in all order to materialize this book. A sincere thanks to all of our friends for encouraging and supporting us.

And at the last to all our readers, our sincere thanks for choosing us, we assure you to give you the best reading experience and knowledge. It's because of your support and encouragement due to which we have attempted for this herculean task.

2020 was not just a year but for each one us it was a year to recall our values. We all were fighting with an invisible enemy who came not only to destroy the beautiful creations but to damage our way of life and to force us to be in captivity. But it failed and helped us to reinvent the purpose for which we are here "To make the Earth more Beautiful".

Tryst with the Pandemic is an attempt to focus on the various issues that appear scary and reflect the predicament of the migrant workers who even did not have a hand to mouth existence. Here is an attempt to showcase the conflict between COVID-19 and people's conviction to win over. We have made an attempt through few reports and write-ups the situation analysis to a larger audience. Thus emphasizing the concept of Vasudeva Kutumbakam and take responsibility to save the humans.

FOREWORD

"The world is not going to be the same again."
The most feared, believed to be omnipresent novel corona virus has physically isolated man, the social animal from rest of the world. Borders were closed between nations and doors & windows closed in neighborhoods. The panic-stricken people were hooked on to television and social media which fed the virus into their minds. For many of them, this is the first time experiencing of "doing nothing and watching detached". However, this passive recess of human kind awakens the nature to replay its original beauty, fragrance of flowers, songs of the birds, lightness of the breeze and the eternal bliss.
On the other hand, it is a health crisis, economic crisis and existentialistic crisis. In the long journey, human race survived many such disasters with extinction of several species. In this covid pandemic too, we have lost the finest minds of our times, celebrated artists, dedicated health workers and millions of fellow human beings. We are entering into a completely new phase of our journey with new treaty with nature.

In this context, thinkers, economists, scientists, technologists, politicians and writers foresee the post–covid world in their own perspectives. The green shoots of optimism are visible already. This book authored by one of the youngest writers Akarshak is such an attempt to understand the impact of covid and look forward towards renewed terms. He has articulated his insights very well. Akarshak along with Dr. Swayam Prabha has understood and presented their untampered views. These suggestions deserve deliberations by the relevant people and that would be the true encouragement to the Authors and their fellow young minds.

-Subbiah Bharathi
Professor

INTRODUCTION

6 January 2021

It was a bright sunny morning of March 14, 2020, after spending the memorable week in Coonoor, when I returned to my campus in Chennai. I was a little upset as I wanted to spend a few more days in the serenity of Coonoor, but I can't compromise my commitments towards my work. Around 1 in the afternoon when I went to meet Dr. N Kannan sir, my HoD, I witnessed a strange atmosphere, was stressful. I was aware that all the events that I planned were cancelled due to some unidentified spread of Virus in foreign nations as well as in my country. Kannan Sir – my Dean – informed me that our fest was also cancelled and before I could ask anything more, he hurriedly left for the meeting. The rumors were in air that our college is also going to declare holiday as a precautionary measure. Next day evening, I was sitting with my friends and we were discussing if College declares a holiday, whether to have another visit to Coonoor or to return to our native. The discussion was progressing without any conclusion when we got a mail and from March 16, 2020 the rumor turned to be correct, our college also declared 15 days of holiday. I was still confused, when I got a sudden call from Swayam Prabha madam my mentor, to discuss about one event I registered for in her college; while speaking I told her I got 15 days of leave and I will able to finish my work. She told me it's better to be in native as we were not aware of this virus and insisted me to return. After finishing the call, when I went inside I had already prepared my mind to return to native and took permission from my parents to return. My mother as usual was happy indeed and my father, who never compromised with my education, I thought it would be difficult to manage him, but he too agreed and allowed me to return perhaps he predicted the intensity of this pandemic. When I conveyed my will to my friends, majority in the room had already decided to return while others opted to wait for a few more days.

The very next day when I was returning back, I got some instructions, wear mask and to keep sanitizer in the airport. Finally, after 4 hours of journey when I returned to my house, I was again engulfed by my memories. But that 15 days holiday would turn into a yea-long holiday we didn't think of.

Today, almost after a year when I am going to Chennai, I am trying to habituate in this new normal. All around people are wearing mask and maintaining social distancing norms. Flights were yet to normalize and still colleges waiting to reopen. I called Swayam Prabha madam. This time it was not a surprise. By the year end we are contributing to a Research Foundation and shared a common vision. Together we contributed and hosted hundreds of events during last year. But that year wasn't normal. When the lockdown was announced we perhaps thought things will be manageable, but as 2020 came to an end, the scenario was completely different, with new learning and few devastating moments which one couldn't imagine. Several businesses were forced to shut, thousands lost their jobs, lakhs of people died and hands joined in prayer across the globe. We witnessed how education shifted from offline to online. And even without moving out of the house, our life continued. Several people were separated from their families and the entire world came to a standstill but we were thankful to God for being safe and could enhance our creativity. The present scenario calls for a thorough understanding of the issues of the grim situation that we have encountered. It will not be wrong to say that we are amidst an emergency situation specifically health hazard that has put the world to a standstill hitting upon the psychology health and economy of the nations.

The outbreak of this pandemic across the globe is a major concern for all. India is also facing this challenge of preventing the virus outbreak and through some of its strict measures able to contain the virus to some extent. This pandemic has brought a series of transformation among people. This book tries to analyze the current situation of corona virus spread in India along with the impact of various measures taken for it. This book has revisited the situation which brought about a metamorphosis in the work culture and measures that is taken. It was observed that the growth rate of infected cases has been controlled with the help of National Lockdown; however, some uncontrolled mass level events had negatively impacted the infected cases. Nevertheless, a situation, as this, is always grueling for people and administration. Despite all odds, there were situations where the education sector, the economic sector did suffer certain issues, but nevertheless, it was a great learning curve for all those involved. As its said *necessity is the mother of invention* and this situation has brought all of us in a single platform of Digitalization.

This book will also be favorable for the common man to introspect not only of India but also of other countries to consider various aspects related to the control of COVID-19 outspread in different regions. The COVID-19 outbreak is a lesson for us all. It is a catastrophe like no other, neither happened in the past nor will continue to happen in the future. We cannot prevent dangerous viruses from emerging, but we should prepare to dampen their dreadful effects on society. One cannot neglect how severe the effect of the current outbreak is on global economy, and not a single country is unaffected. But this not only has consequences on the economy but it has affected all the sectors of the society, which has led to dramatic changes in how businesses act and consumers behave. However, not to forget that it has also bought changes where people have learned to be self-dependent instead of being restraint in enhancing their economic standards. This book makes an effort to address some of the pandemic-related issues affecting society. The number of operational places and events conducted during lockdown data has been analyzed through news reports and channels. Based on the news reports, the major events were traced and people getting infected due to such events have been covered from the Indian data repository created using crowd sourcing channels. Corona virus is the first pandemic of the 21st century, of this scope where we have known the complete information about the mutation and the place of its origin from the very start. With social distancing in place, herd immunity building and collaborative work underway to develop treatments and a vaccine. It can be related to economic crisis what we saw in 1929. 1.6 billion workers stand in verge of losing their job says, International Labor Organization. Let's contribute to save the one Planet we got.

CONTENT

Is Covid-19 the Beginning or the End of Globalization?

With bans on international flights and travel restrictions imposed, this pandemic has put mankind in shackles. The social distancing norms have forced us to keep safe distance between people, but take a look at the epicenter of this virus outbreak, it's the most visited cities. Cities, which are backbone of economy or of industries, and cities that welcomed globalization showed their worst impact in this pandemic. This has caused the sharpest decline in international travels after World War 2.

Globalization represents the progress of mankind. Globalization allows for the development of the societies and backward classes, it allows to share culture, knowledge, and today. It is a process which carries out a transformation of societies by binding them together and expanding economical or cultural activities across the globe. Globalization allows the nations to remain connected, to help each other in this crisis. Truly in India we say VASUDHEVA KUTTUMBAKAM – the world is our home. However, this has resulted in a crisis. This provided a smooth passage for the Virus to spread, to bring disaster to humankind. The current crisis has reflected the negative side. But as we sailed forward, nations joined forces to fight, they vowed to defeat this. The globalization approached due to the Industrial Revolution in the 20th century – as revolution allowed production of goods and to use them on a large scale, and rise in population created demand for goods. Many western countries saw this as a chance to enrich their resources. As the western countries started colonizing the Asia and African states, the spread of culture and religion took place, thus strengthening the globalization. With the invention of steam engine, it reduced the cost of transportation both internationally and inland.

After World War II, several nations marched towards economic growth by reducing the restrictions. The formation of the United Nations and various associated organizations provided a framework for the countries to trade agreements and settle disputes.

As the aviation sector has become affordable and open, sky treaties helped to bring markets and people together. The growth of internet ensures people across the globe to work more freely and from anywhere.

Globalization has spread rapidly through the expansion of democracy and free ideologies.

The economic crisis that has destroyed the world after Covid-19 pandemic has led us to search more questions about globalization. We are commenting whether the pandemic would end or open up a new chapter.

The uncertainties about the future of globalization arose because of the lockdown that has caused all major economies to shut.

In December 2019, the first confirmed case about the virus was reported in Wuhan, China still unknown. By January, the number rose to 7000 confirmed cases across 19 countries. By March, several thousands of people were dead, and lakhs were infected. Countries were

under lockdown as the cases continue to rise. Every single country recorded cases of Covid-19.
If we compare this with Spanish flu, we can see that Spanish flu lasted for 2 years and infected 500 million people, which are around 5% of the world's population at that time. The four successive waves resulted over million dead worldwide. But the rate of spread percentage was relatively slow and several states remain untouched, whereas Covid cases are about 33 million but it has spread to almost all nations within a few months.

So if we say that Covid pandemic is the end of globalization, it would be wrong. In recent months, we saw attempts to view the challenges that the process of globalization faced from several different entities, this pandemic turned to be manmade. Well, I won't say whether it is manufactured in a Lab in Wuhan, but I would say lack of coordination in handling the situation or delaying in considering it to be serious resulted in this massive disaster. So blaming globalization is useless. There are several benefits of globalization – globalization connects producers and consumers, it provides a bigger market and helps in reducing the monopoly profits by handful of Capitalists.
It enhances the growth and helps many developing countries to fasten their economic growth. Several nations sent huge relief to nations and helped them to fight with poverty and diseases. We have seen humanitarian efforts in Africa, how the world joined hands to uproot terrorism. Another advantage is that the free movement of labor between countries. Several workers go to gulf nations to work to support their

infrastructure development. We gain from the sharing of ideas and skills across the borders.
Opening of markets allows developing countries to borrow money from international funds and Government join hands to strengthen bilateral relations.
But this pandemic has stopped this process, as several lakhs lost their jobs and they are returning to their home state but we have also witnessed how leader joined hand and hold Annual Summit of the United Nations. Countries are marching together to find a permanent solution, vaccine. Countries are helping each other to defeat this Red Virus.

The sad aspect of globalization was that major economies have been showing signs of getting cut off from the global economy and they started focusing on their own issues. The exports in 2020 could fall to a level last seen during wars – that would be a serious painful fall, especially for developing nation whose economy depends on world economy. As the international travel collapsed, the tourism sector that contributes more to economy witnessed a serious fall. As of May, every nation had imposed partial or complete lockdown thus restrictions on international travel, that means a complete no to foreign visitors.
If you ask me, how this globalization will be in post–covid world, then, when the pandemic will come under control the same trend will. Well, in 2020, it is likely to be Low.
The key lesson that we got is that globalization in happy days grows faster, and in bad times they shrink faster.

Only few countries around the world are self-reliant on the various e-commerce and video conferencing applications boomed by Covid-19 thus connecting people worldwide. The transfer of technology made this a key to success.

In conclusion, Covid-19 may look like a "No to Globalization" but without globalization, until and unless a nation becomes self-reliant, it can't fight alone as "Together we stand, divided we fall". Countries should work together, should fight together. With proper management and sharing of information pandemic like this could be avoided. That's what globalization truly means, a thread that binds all nation together. It should generate an idea, our countries' should not be our identity, Humanity is our identity. No nation, No race or creed, but we are resident of Earth, if we able to bring this type of hypothetical community we can stop this crisis to happen again in future.

Need for a Common Curriculum in Post–Covid World?

The school education in India can be broadly classified into three boards – CBSE, ICSE and State boards. There are around 40 boards in India, educating around 130 million students. But the problem is these boards have different curriculums, which does not deliver uniform knowledge, thus creates a Gap. The Constitution guarantees *Right to Education* but nowadays quantity has superseded the quality. As there is no uniform curriculum the different boards have different percentage of students, thus few students are lagging behind. I will not name the board, but in my college, I have found certain students found it difficult to understand the lectures, though the faculties use understandable English. Even when they write in exam, they are not able to understand and feel outmatched in any competition. I would rather blame politics as regional parties to shine their fortune play the language card or regional card. They claim that Common curriculum is a threat to diversity. As a result, no government has taken any prominent steps to make this system uniform.

Several countries have a common curriculum throughout the nation, this is to ensure equal opportunity for everyone. But in India, states like West Bengal have banned English for several years, so in this competitive world, is it possible to keep an entire generation out of such a relevant subject? You can find a wide difference in curriculum of English language between ICSE Board and State Board. ICSE board has a perfectly good standard of English, while State Boards have a moderate standard. English is not only the case; in fact, the standard of curriculum in science and mathematics is also of clashing contrast.

The education should be free of politics as in some cases, political influence is harmful for an education system. Some states have reservations of nearly 80% of the seats for domicile students, this is quite common in state run universities, with a common syllabus neither the political, like the one we are seeing in NEET. A common curriculum will provide no discrimination and provide unbiased platform for all the students.

Today, all of us are engaged in a race, a race for marks and grades. We are running behind the numbers and ignoring the quality. Different boards have different curriculum and a different standard of difficulties too. A student may score good marks in boards but when they will sit for national level exams they may land up into problems.

In this post–covid world when globalization is a factor, there should be a common curriculum all over the nation, at least 60% should be common. This will help all the students to be on par with education.

The objectives of the *Right to Education Act* are to provide free and compulsory education to every child but it should also ensure quality education.

“Pen is more powerful than sword” we are familiar with this phrase, but when we are fighting for uniform civil law, or one nation one election, one nation one card we should also raise our voice for One Nation One Education Board. Education is the key that can drive a nation towards greater peaks. Think if a single pen can change the world what lakhs of pen will do.

Different Boards follows different pattern, different curriculum, and during this pandemic, we all thought why different boards are walking differently. The need for a common board thus becomes a necessity after this pandemic. We believe in equality of opportunities and this can be the first step to ensure that.

Education is in concurrent list, which means both State and Union can make laws according to their need. Therefore, some states are regionalizing the education rather than nationalizing them. But as a citizen of a diverse nation, we should have complete knowledge about the diversity, about the social and cultural aspects of the entire country. Education plays a pivotal role in development of a student. Education provides opportunity to all. The different boards with different syllabus and schooling provoke inequality among students. As per a study, rural student prefers state board while urban population prefers centralized Boards like CBSE or ICSE, and in fact, there is a proverb "Rich prefers ICSE, middle Class prefers CBSE and Poor goes to state board". But I think we shouldn't have this kind of mentality as how education is for all, in other words, let this nation have a single education board that will govern the entire system, which will provide equal opportunity.

Various colleges have various types of syllabus, introduction of NEET and National Testing Agency is a good step on how student will get equal chances.

The Indian Government spends around % GDP on Education while several others spending around 8 to 6% on education. In fact, the country is in a serious shortage of teachers. And a single teacher is over burdened with work so how will they dedicate their best to student? Few states like Tamil Nadu and Kerala pay huge attention to education while few don't. If your seed is defected, then how the fruit will be healthy?

I come from the school Kendriya Vidyalaya, which has same syllabus as almost all infrastructures, same uniform and same prayer. It runs 1225 schools in India and 3 in abroad with around 13 lakhs members. Schools like Jawahar Navodaya Vidayalaya, Army Public School or Delhi Public School, which run chains of school across the Nation, promote common curriculum system. This is what promotes unity and integrity of our Nation.

These differences in learning gap between the students from various boards create confusion as, during higher studies, most of the students aren't able to accommodate in case they switch schools affiliated to other boards. They may face problem in terms of adapting new curriculum and system.

After this pandemic, when different states or more accurately when different education boards have different opinions, think for a moment, is that promoting equal opportunity? Few boards have been awarded number of core subjects while few provided moderate. No one knows whether this year's result will get equal weightage in future or not.

A common curriculum could have saved India's Education system in this pandemic.

Now, let us take a look at how this can be done. If we make the general subjects common and introduce a subject on Cultural importance of that state along with choices of what languages we can accept, then we may even have a common curriculum. Students can have a common language and a common subject if they wish to skip state based subject. This is what I mean when I say we can have a common curriculum across the nation, which is indeed important today.

Paradigm shift in teaching and learning

The first picture that engulfs our mind whenever we hear the word "Classroom" is of students sitting together under one roof with a teacher holding a piece of chalk and scribbling on the black board. It is evident to have such a scenario in our mind as we are familiar with this type of system, systematically schools start usually with a regular morning assembly or Prayer. Usually, the classes begin with the bells going off as you mark the beginning of another chapter in your Book of Memories. But today's scenario is quite different, no more morning assemblies and classes ending with a stale popup, "meeting ended by the Host". No queues for submitting assignments, no red marks on notebooks and memories aren't adding up the way they used to. What we've actually got is an extraordinarily stale school experience right from your drawing room.

"Time and Tide Wait for None". We are passing through an unprecedented scenario where almost every corner of the globe has either complete or partial lockdown. In India, like other countries, restrictions were imposed on outdoor chores with markets and malls closed. The entire country was standing still for 21 days. From December 2019, the world was in a state of emergency and a global healthcare crisis. Millions were already dead and several others across the periphery of nations were suffering, every country was on pause.

Although time didn't stop for anyone, it kept on flowing with each passing day. We had no progress, no growth. "Can a developing country like India afford Zero work or Zero Progress in this competitive day and age?" Well to remain alive is a primal priority today, but to keep everything running is a necessity to have a better future. We hope to get the vaccine soon; several nations are reopening the business and loosening the restrictions. The offices are reopening, hotels are getting booked, but the schools are still waiting for their pride to return, corridors are waiting for them to run and classrooms bored and tired of being quarantine center waiting for the classes to start again.

A transition from "Work in office" to "Work from home" culture is something that we restrained ourselves in the past, but this pandemic brought a new culture, in spite of having "Classes in School" we are having "Classes online". Thanks to digitization that provided an alternative. It is true that no parents will ever take the risk of sending their children to school, at least they will have to wait till the vaccine is out, but on the other hand, they can't compromise their future. So as the year rolled on to September, online classes became a necessity and invaded the regular classes.

The irony is those who joined school for the first time or took admission in colleges across the nation, "Students are yet to see their Campuses and meet their friends with whom they will create their memories".

There can be an hour-long debate between distance classes and online classes but nowadays we are facing a new kind of argument between online and offline mode of studies. Recent advancement in the field of technology has made it possible to hold or conduct classes and meetings online. However, one cannot neglect how much online classes are competent. The history of regular classes can be traced back to several centuries ago, where we adapted "Gurukul" system of education, which is boarding cum education center. Definitely, the primary focus was on one-to-one education. We have always come across pictures depicting "guru" with his "sishayas". This type of culture is way too similar to that of regular classes. Well, one may always argue unavailability of technology in those days, but for a moment think, do you feel comfortless in online classes? Are you able to create any special bond? Most importantly, are you making memories?

Let me begin with traditional classes, the average ratio between faculties and student is 1:60. So simply by seeing faces, faculties can tell whether the students are attentive or not as the faculties are well experienced and versatile. I remember how my math faculty used to treat me because I never remained attentive in their classes, but honestly, today when I look back I thank them because at least I passed my examinations because of them.

In online classes we are seeing the same content, but in school days, we used to have rotation so once in a week we used to sit in the front row which was a very pathetic scenario for backbenchers, as they have to remain extra attentive.

There were few faculties who deliver their best in classrooms as on several occasions I have found that teachers deliver their knowledge to a class based on their personal mood and average knowledge percentage. Average knowledge percentage is quite an interesting thing. Suppose there are two sections of class 10, section A and Section B with 15 students each. Section A has 8 students with more than 90% in assessment and 7 students with average 70%, while section B has 4 students with more than 90% in assessment and 11 students with average of 70%. It will be quite noticeable that the difference in teaching methodology of the same faculty in these two sections. The question may remain the same, but the way they will deliver the concepts will be different. No, I won't say this is biasness, but this is what students need – a customized learning system. Even though this can be done through online mode also but the point to which it all boils down to is "MOOD". Sometimes, faculties used to take extra classes either by cancelling games period or by occupying an extra free period. One can easily understand the emotions attached especially with games period. So at that point of time, faculties understand our feelings yet they try their level best to make fruitful outcome from that. It is just their ability to bring about a change.

A complete new methodology "online classes" with online submission of assignments and attendance through collector, but further along the way, we failed to

recognize the importance of an ongoing system, because deep down we cannot replace regular mode.
At this point of time to remain safe and to continue the progress, there are no alternatives. The universities have conferred online degrees conducted through online admissions, started classes too, but are teachers are able to teach us freely? Or is it that the students aren't able to concentrate?

Many students may have problems in their families; this may have an impact on their mood, so how can we expect a fruitful outcome? Online classes don't provide an equal opportunity. You can say, everyone can experience the same by seeing the common screen but the refutation to this point is not so easy. There are several who still cannot afford a smart phone, there are thousands living in areas with a low bandwidth, or in other words, they have poor network. Is it justifying to march ahead while leaving them behind? Someone's father or mother may have health issues or they could be frontline fighters in this pandemic, risking their lives to save others. Think about the mental stress the student will have. If he or she would have been to school, at least his or her friends will be there, to uplift their mood. Ignoring the cost of data packs, there can be technical glitches; also every time we ask the same thing again and again, is this called providing equal opportunity to everyone?
This is new experience that we got, a complete online mode of education. From admission to classes, from placement drives to conferring degrees, from webinars to conferences but even though with the personal bond

between faculties and students and the happiness of making new friends or the feelings of visiting a new place, there are things which we are really missing.

This paradigm shift should be reversed soon…

Effect of Covid-19 on the Society?

As this Pandemic provoked to be one of the most terrible catastrophes in India, in the month of April, we witnessed one of the biggest "Ghar wapsi". Thousands of laborers vacated cities to save themselves from starvation. This ghar wapsi occurred when the migrant population returned to their forgotten lands, when corona virus engulfed the nation, lockdown was imposed to curtail the spread of this deadly virus. Factories and workplaces shutdown and millions of worker became jobless. They lost their income and forced to live amid of a pandemic with shortage of resources and uncertainty about their future states that never adopted them, neither welcomed them, even with half-opened arms. As a result, they started their unplanned journey towards their native, and in some cases, perhaps they are returning to their hometown for the first time. This has forced us to reduce the burden of over-population that slowed India's progress by acting as a termite.

It is not only that the poor have suffered. We often fail to recognize the contribution by the Middle class and it would be unjust if I don't mention formal sector employees. As the Nation stood still, offices and workplaces were closed and millions of employees were forced to live on half paid salaries. Think about this class, they can't even beg, neither they can steal. The effect on them is equally intense. The market was on fire. The price of day-to-day commodities was higher than the average, and amid this, pandemic keeping ourselves fit is indeed a major concern. Think about a salaried person earning rupees 50,000 per month, now he is getting only 30000; he has to maintain his standard as best as he can as we humans are slave of our habits. They may have to pay rent, electricity bill and school fees in certain cases and they have to save a certain amount for any sort of emergency. Think about the mental stress, this is a tale of a single India, where we often acknowledge what is visible, what is measurable, but we fail to pay any heed to those which are invisible.

There are approx. 130 million migrant workers in our nation and most belong to eastern Uttar Pradesh, Bihar and West Bengal. Generally, they are daily-wage laborers engaged as construction workers and manufacturing laborers. This sector is often termed as informal sector.

According to the 2011 census, Mumbai has the largest number of migrants followed by Delhi. Neither of them has received any formal education nor do they work under any fixed contracts or job security. They are hired and fired orally.

When corona virus scrubbed the nation, they lost their job overnight, with no money and no public transport available due to lockdown restrictions; we saw thousands of them returning to eastern states mostly, with their families either by walking or my cycling, several thousands of kilometers.

Some families are happy, enjoying their family time. Some families are passing their miserable time as their earner lost job and they rely on limited resources, and there are several thousand others who are on road, fighting to earn daily bread every day.

If you ask me the reason behind this force exodus, I would rather blame the system. As migrants lost jobs, they faced challenges to survive in the cities that used them. Workers faced assault as they were considered to be infected, and upon reaching their hometown, they were projected as the potential carrier of the virus.

Approximately 400 workers died and many were arrested for violating the restrictions. We have witnessed horrific sights when migrants were killed after trains ran over them while they were sleeping on tracks. We have seen the deaths but these stories of migrants are enough to bring tears to our eyes, there are many other such stories yet to hear. The government issued no directives, but according to me, they remain in papers for the fame only. Few States provided facilities and set of thousands of camps to shelter lakhs of workers, but states like Maharashtra put little to negligible effort to stop this exodus. The shocking images of migrants walking on roads in scorching Sun flooded the social media and it exposed the shocking truth about India informal sector. The government's effort to provide one Nation, one ration card had a major impact, as PDS card provided 900 million people this uniform measure. Therefore, for economy, this can be helpful for preventing any such disaster in the future. The government announced Sramik special train with the thought that it will be helpful but the situation worsened when politics induced in Sramik trains, as parties left no stone unturned to shine their fortune. This pandemic turned out to be a disaster because of the lack of data about the informal sector and all the data available on estimation basis. Informal sector is mostly comprised of delivers workers who have no access to social security and live in poverty. If you think about the long-term effect, the labor shortages could have a negative impact, as they may consider whether to return to the cities or to stay back in their natives. If we were to overcome the caste-based treatment, we would have achieved something to an extent. There are approximately 89.9% Urban population who take up casual daily work, and considering an effect that there is a fast majority who are illiterate, but current challenges can be overcome into the winning shot by proper coordination among the state and the center. In another word, we should take them for granted and should never overlook them again, as they play a pivotal role in running the society. The entire nation was on road no matter what the state was, the migrants helped each other to reach their respective destination. Some people were inside their house enjoying the vacation. On the other hand, those who made their life comfortable early on were suffering. If you wish to find any irony it is that, more than 300 deaths were reported because of lockdown and the entire system was quiet.

Amid this crisis, I witness true stories that still disturb my mind sometimes; we should be a little emotional to know the real suffering of the people. The things are different now but the situations are not the same and they probably will never be the same again. Think for a moment, about those families who lost that their dear ones, not because of the virus but because of the mismanagement on taking this pandemic lightly. But this negligence towards migrants and lack of political could create misery in future. We have neglected problems associated with systems and transformations done without planning which has produced such a picture of India. Keeping in mind that this is not a regular phenomenon, this is one-hour future and dear our social–economic progress.

How Covid Pandemic Accelerated the Digital Revolution?

Revolution is just a medium to bring about a change, today we are contributing towards an ongoing revolution. We are not on roads, calling strikes or participating in Bandhs. Neither did we take a chance on Twitter or any other social media platforms. Situation brings out the best revolution and each one of us is contributing, either directly or indirectly. Over the past few months, we have seen businesses closing down, postponement of events, families confined to their house as a deadly virus swept across the world. We have seen how quickly people accommodated themselves and adapted changes, which expedited the process of revolution. To stay connected we have learnt new ways, we have contributed, innovated and brought out new alternatives.

The world started shifting from analog to digital era even before the 21st century could even knock on our doors. On 1990, we recorded only 0.05% of the world's population was using internet and by 2020, 59% population were using various digital technologies, an addition of 4.5 billion users in just 20 years. We have seen how technologies brought our entire market to our drawing room. They brought billions of products in our smart phones and enabled us to buy them, without even leaving our house. Day by day as this pandemic is tearing down the global economy and challenging us, dreaming to conquer humanity. But humanity became more advanced and chose continuity. Digitization provided a substitute so that humanity can move forward without losing its relevance in the present situation. Several unfamiliar words became trending, video conferencing applications witnessed very high downloads. Over the past decade, we have seen a firm transition from "work from office" culture to "work from home" culture. What this epidemic brought to us is a "School from House" culture. Nowadays usual morning assemblies have vanished. "The meeting ended by the Host" is the usual message that pop up to notify us, the end of the class and it's time to rejoin the next class, replacing the more familiar ring of bell. Instead of taking permission to go out, we just turn off our videos and to cover our mistakes, we blame the network signal. The usual lunch break with friends is replaced with lunch with families. No red mark on notebooks and no queue for submitting assignments. With colleges closed, students are more dependent on internet; they prefer online internships as companies are providing online training. Various institutes have started online certification courses. But the worst effected crowd according to me are those who are doing research, as research centers are closed there are no alternatives available for various scientific equipment housed in the centers.

But take a break and think for those who cannot afford smart phones or laptop or even data packs, so how can we call this as a successful revolution?

No one can predict what's coming, we can't neglect the fact that every year there was a significant growth in the digitizing of our nation, this pandemic just came out of the blue and affected us all, but it accelerated the growth of digitization.

Amazon and Netflix witnessed about 60% growth with 16 million new sign ups on Netflix as on April 22. For the universities and colleges, the traditional convocations are replaced with E-Convocations to confer the degrees. To assure everyone a job, they started online placement drives. This is what a revolution should do – to offer a substitute before calling for a change. Situation brings change, change brings revolution. Several thousands of people were not familiar with Zoom platform; they were not aware as to how a Google form is created or a meeting is hosted. They were new to the concept of Google classroom but situation urged them to learn, to adapt new things.

As paper or printed material could be the potential carriers of the virus, several newspaper agencies focused more on digital newspaper. Many people started avoiding cash and opted safer platforms like G-Pay or Phone-Pe which had significant growth after the monetization.

With religious places closed due to restrictions and limitation to the number of invitees, will we be asked to attend an online wedding of my cousin? Thanks to digital platforms, even in this lockdown in spite of having barriers we got somewhat of a real time experience. As darshans were closed, Temples also provided E-Dashing facilities by going live on social media.

Healthcare sector proved to be a giant killer in this pandemic, while various hospitals started online consultancy services, this sector contributed the most. Due to the unavailability of transportation, though clinics were open, doctors chose online mode to deliver their best effort in curing the patients.

As the Coronavirus continues to spread around the world, governments have put restrictions on the movement of people, the functioning of services and rules on physical distancing. Within this context, technology can have a profound effect on citizen's daily lives and ensure them access to health services, access to information, attend schools and continue their growth.

Many sectors are still away from digitization and need boost but it becomes quite clear that this pandemic has catalyzed a pivotal change in our day-to-day life. This has pushed us forward to learn new technologies, refinement and adoption of changes. I believe, these alternatives will continue to stay even after the pandemic is over.

Hence, it is quite enough to accept that we are in the amidst of an accelerated digital revolution.

A Conflict within self and a gateway to resolve the conflict.

In this period of COVID-19, the whole world has come to a halt and humans being locked in their homes, the time has now come for us to resolve our conflicts from home. All the while we were complaining of pressures and commitments in our academic and professional lives keeping us occupied and preventing us from spending time with our dear and near ones. Yet now when time has bestowed us infinity at our doorsteps, we crib and grumble about our ties with our intimate bonds. What does this suggest? Does this hint that all this while we have actually been in a world of illusion? In fact, we as individuals always look forward to a world where we delve into a willing suspension of disbelief. Why is it that we fail in having a conversation for straight five minutes without it ending up in an argument within the home itself? It's a matter of concern that most of the time we don't rely on our conversations rather are glued to our cell phones which most of the time creates a virtual world. But on the contrary, it is also because of the device one gets closer to the world though virtually. The pertinent question is, can we deal and thrive harmoniously with our near and dear ones in this technological world? Few measures are suggested to fight the battle within.

1. Being emotionally balanced

Keeping an account of our physiological responses and our behavioral actions can help us to identify our emotions and consciously choose to avoid certain factors that may lead to an upheaval of emotions. We need to make a balance between our IQ and ESQ. (Intelligent Quotient and Emotional Quotient)

2. Being empathetic

Empathy is something that we fail to share with people who are in need of it. If we understand the current situation, we would realize that we are faced with the depression theory and suicides. We are driven by inhibitions against the individual when he encounters with the disease. And surprisingly, individuals hide their infection as they feel they will be socially excluded. So, we need to pay attention to mood changes and signs of distress that people in our country are facing in the present surroundings experience. Be sensitive to the emotions of our near and dear ones and offer them a word of cheer, a shoulder to rest. We have to judiciously use the language and pacify so that it makes people socially inclusive.

3. Understanding is the shortest distance between people

Lending our ears open to the concerns of others with a heart that does not prejudge or with suspended judgment. At this juncture, we should understand the psychology of the people and make them comfortable to be accommodative with the feeling of belongingness.

4. Giving credibility

The pandemic has bought a devastating upon the every individual who feel left out and find themselves in a grim situation perplexed with thoughts which never would have touched them when situation was normal. Taking interest in understanding the costs and giving credibility to any sort of contribution that they make might not cost anything but plays a very important role in comforting the individuals. Appreciate with gratefulness the efforts and expertise of the people that lead to our harmonious existence.

5. Being approachable as we know sharing is caring

Being responsible and to contribute whatever little you can by being amicable is to ensure a sense of unity and cohesiveness to people who are fighting within themselves during this crisis.

6. Time is the precious gift given to anyone

Lending an ear to the people and talk of the golden olden days, play games and learn and unlearn something together, giving the strength to withstand what lies ahead.

7. Being technically updated

Technology is indeed one of the engaging devices which can bring revolution in the world and is keeping us connected and sensible during this time, where we have no other means of staying in touch with our friends and acquaintances. We should take the time to show care and concern to others through a simple emoticon, sharing a something which would make one feel associated.

It's easy to get swayed away up in the media about COVID-19. Every day we regularly look into our phones, watching the news, and trying to update ourselves pandemic memes across social media sites.
Though we understand knowledge is power, but on the contrary, it is a matter of concern that is knowledge about covid is really enhancing our knowledge or confining us more into thoughtful and grim condition.
It is going to be odd source of good news and positivity to people around instead of adding to anyone's voes

Developing Resilience in Children

Global concerns about the consequences of disasters, political violence, disease, malnutrition, maltreatment, and other life threats to human progress and well-being have made an upsurge to work on building resilience. This one points out the progress and issues in research that aims to understand adverse experiences and human adaptation to it. There are few questions that are to be considered: Why is the need for global research on resilience important? And why is it important to develop resilience? And after Covid-19, these questions became more prominent. The reason being human beings are exposed to so many variations that they need to develop resilience. The development of children around the globe is threatened by disasters, political violence, pandemics, and other adversities that can have life-changing consequences for individuals, families, and the future of the societies. The beginning of the 21st century was started by a horrifying sequence of events affecting large numbers of victims across the world. These include terror attacks, hurricanes, tsunami in the Indian Ocean triggered by one of the largest earthquakes in human history, the BP Oil Spill in the Gulf of Mexico and many such catastrophic incidents. United Nations' report suggests that millions of children each year are victim of disasters, as a result many are displaced.

These adversities have raised global concerns about the endangered children as well as the future of societies, while also reflecting a lack of preparedness to handle such calamities. These concerns have given rise to international agencies search for evidence and guidance on what helps to minimize risk and promote resistance to face these threats to human life. It is through the development of self-efficacy and resilience one will be able to face it.

Resilience is a broad umbrella, covering many concepts related to positive patterns of adapting in the context of adversity. The concept of resilience encompasses phenomena where one when develops it has the ability to adapt a system that has been threatening by experiences capable of disrupting or destroying the successful operations of the system. The idea of resilience can be applied to any functional system, it has been applied most frequently to individuals as living systems and less often to higher level social systems, including families, classrooms, and schools. Thus, if one identifies a child as resilient, who has the qualities of three things – I can, I have and I will – two judgments have been made: this child too meet expectations for positive adaptation and it has been a significant contribution to the adaptation of the child to the turbulent environment. Lois Murphy noted long ago that the adaptive quality of a living system has two aspects: adapting to the environment, what she called Coping I, and maintaining internal integration, termed Coping II. In the lives of children, there have been many criteria for external adaptation, ranging from school achievement to getting along with peers; and also criteria for internal adaptation, such as psychological well-being or physical health. One of the most important contributions of the early resilience researchers in behavioral sciences was their attention to the criteria is to develop coping mechanisms and which will bring about positive adaptation. It is observed that defining positive adaptation in children that focused on the effective behavior expected for children in multiple domains of achievement; these expectations varied over the course of development, as well as across cultural and historical contexts.

The Role of Self-Efficacy in Promoting Resilience

The most important protective factor that has received limited research attention is self-efficacy, this attribute is the focus of the present study. Albert Bandura (1981, 1983, 1999) has been a pioneer in self-efficacy research and Bandura has conceptualized self-efficacy as individuals' beliefs in their capabilities to mobilize the motivation, cognitive resources, and agency to exert control over a given event. It is the belief in one's capabilities to produce a certain outcome or goal that is seen as the foundation of human agency (Bandura, Pastorelli, Barbaranelli & Caprara, 1999).

While facing adverse events, those who believe that they will be able to exert control over their thoughts are more likely to persevere in their efforts. Those who are self-efficacious are more likely to reject negative thoughts about themselves or their abilities than those with a sense of personal inefficacy (Ozer & Bandura, 1990). One central aspect of an individual's self-efficacy is the belief that through the exertion of control one can influence the outcome of events in one's life. Other investigators of resilience chose to include emotional health in their defining criteria. Developmental task theory, which emerged in the mid-20th century, has been refined as a result of this recent attention, and a number of its propositions put to empirical test. Among few of the conclusions supported by the researchers are the following: (1) Adaptation to the environment is a salient feature of development periods to forecast success in this pandemic situation. Building competence is another essential trait to build resilience. (2) Interventions to promote success in these tasks had preventive effects on behavioral and emotional problems.

Existence of God in Covid World

It is true that for the past many years existence of the God has fascinated the humans the most and after the pandemic hit the world the question became more prominent. Why God let this pandemic to happen?

It would be useless to indulge in the debate over the existence of God. But rather we should try to find the real meaning of the God. I am neither a scientist nor someone who could find it out. We all believe in God, try to offer our prayers and fulfilling rituals using various methods. If we realize and question ourselves is it required and what are we up to? Only because he is the Supreme Being or because he has the ability to bring miracles.

I remember one incident, when I was in my class 11, one of my friends met with an accident while we were on going to school. When we took him to the hospital with the help of a local resident, the doctors gave an ultimatum, about his faint chances of survival. I remember how much devastated his family were on that and so we were. Everyone around me started praying. Some were calling Allah, some were praying to Jesus while we kept calling Shiva. And today when the entire world is facing the dreadful effect of Covid-19, people across the globe have joined hands in praying to Almighty. They are keeping their faith high on the God they believe, they trust. They believe All Mighty The Supreme Power will protect them.

I believe that the Creation of the human being is still the biggest mystery. We all are composite creature who needs a base for their success. Probably that's the main reason why we started worshipping God. If you ask somebody that, have you seen God? Their answer will be simply no. then why we go to temple to worship them?
It's a well-established fact that 4600 million years ago by Big Bang the universe was created. Gradually, in the Earth, all living beings came into existence. But different mythologies and different religions describe the creation of universe in a different way but till now we are not able to reveal the truth nor we have been able to prove the existence of God. But I have a firm belief that God exists not as a God we see, we worship but a spirit that control guard the universe. And after the disruption the pandemic created that some people may curse their fate as to God didn't protect them. But on the contrary, one has to realize that it is because we were taught a lesson through this that we disturbed the Creator's manifestation of beauty The Nature. We disrupted the ecological balance so God has a way to teach us.

Going inside we see an idol that's what we call God. But God has a much deeper meaning – a meaning beyond our capacity to understand. In fact, in today's ever changing world, we find our connection to God.
According to Hindus Lord Brahma was created by Adi parashakti. It was Brahma who further created the Earth, created humans and animal. Islam mythology claims that Allah created and various other religions have their own point of view. In Christianity too it is a power a holy

power governs the Earth. But according to my point of view, there is a sprit which governs the Earth, which exists, long time we did and will continue to exist. Actually in terms of science, it is an energy which is limitless. Over the centuries, the power had increased. We all are aware of the popular law "energy can neither be created nor destroyed", its power is so much that till now no device has been invented to measure such a huge amount of power. The evidence that supports my view is that scientist Satyendranath Bose has discovered God particle even Albert Einstein believe that God exists. The universe & the vacuum energy creates it. The Ancient sages describe Kali as the Dark Energy & Lalita to be vacuum who later through a cosmic egg gave birth to the universe. The electron forms various shapes, figures. The electrons are omnipresent it is Omni force so it's our mind which created such type of figures. But the energy is there which is controlling us. Judaism keeps distant from the creator God. However, Hinduism divides it into Sagun & Nirgun. Saguna is the present form of God particle that Dr. Bose had discovered. The electrons or the energy store in it is indestructible, it is who govern, the universe. The sagun a form is shapeless just like the electrons. The worshippers of Brahma worship his saguna form they worship Kendra bindhu.

today when so much restlessness resides in our heart, when we are so afraid of that Virus. When nothing we created can protect us I believe by putting all our focus on what we want, we can achieve an energy just as by meditation we try to control our body, it helps us to live in consciousness, it helps to keep our body calm. Day and night our scientists are trying their level best to find the vaccine and are successful. Doctors and healthcare staffs are fighting to save the precious life of human beings. They are the God in real life. For me the concept of God is very clear it is a power that governs us. God is nothing but a sprit; it is an energy it develops by our own development. The spirit the energy is omnipresent it is indestructible. It is limit less. It is the energy who creates the universe, & it will be responsible for its destruction. Everything is destined and everything that happens is for a good cause. We understand Covid has destroyed life of many but it also has a positive side. It has opened the gate of opportunities. There is so much to know so much to learn. It's our responsibility to turn the situation in our favor. Covid-19 is a man-made disaster that could be avoided. But alongside the Almighty has gifted us so many other things, God was there with us, with each one of us fighting for us and guarding our souls. It would be useless to say that God doesn't exist by just one incident. We fail to recognize its potential because it is beyond our capacity to understand.

Is There Any Role of Religion in Covid World?

In this planet, each one of us belongs to a particular religion. There are many religions, but what are these for? A religion is a group who follows a particular God, follows a particular tradition and perform certain rituals. It is true that today religion is dividing people, the bloodshed in the name of God is spreading but Covid made us understand, God didn't expect this. In covid world there has been instances when various religious communities came forward to help other religion. We humans are responsible for creating religion and that makes us separate. Some have done this only for their own benefits. Religion divides a man on the basis of caste, community, culture. We all live in the same planet. We share common land, air and water, then why should we have different religions when our objectives are same, when we share common vision – a common vision to make the world Covid free, a world without mask and endless hugs. For God we all are his children; he never creates any discrimination among us. He loves us all, equally. Not only we divide people based on religion but also on the basis of caste. From the past many centuries, Brahmins are responsible for worship, Khastriya for war, Vyas & Sudras for other different works. Now tell me if a child wants to give something to his mother to eat, what he will be called? He will love, to do it with his tiny hand so God is our father and our mother, then why we ask Brahmins to offer food? We do not need to depend on others to prove our love towards God. They can read our soul. There is a thought God help those who help themselves. The spirit takes shape and size as we want him to do. It is the sprit that we claim us a God. God wants us to maintain Harmony, to live in peace. We all live in this Earth. We should have brotherhood and not to forget our main religion, Humanity. This Covid period made us understood the importance of humanity. We should love each other, help each other. This fight is not of any single nation nor of any particular religion. This fight is of us all. It is for us to save the one planet we got.

Conclusion

The thought of this book brought ripples in our minds as the pandemic situation was aptly mind boggling. We are juxtaposed with various apprehensions that what would be the impact of this catastrophe on Globalization. The thought of this book brought ripples in my mind as the pandemic situation was aptly mind boggling. This pandemic has started a new phase of anti-Globalization Sentiments, but the leaders should reshape the world where both Globalization and cultural entity can be preserved. Moreover, we have seen how divested this pandemic was, and standing to this point, we all should pledge to protect the Planet we got. Across the Globe, we have witnessed how much we all are divided; this Pandemic made us realize that *Divided We fall*, once again. Covid-19 was a war, a war with an invisible enemy, a war that was fought by all nations together and millions have sacrificed their lives. This is our chance to fight back, let the free voice and free mind reach every corner of the world. The key argument is that the current crisis will fundamentally change key economic actors' risk appetite, triggering a renewed risk assessment that will lead to the comeback of buffers and borders across industries. This partial return to regionalization will involve a form of de-globalization that transforms modern just-in-time management into its just-in-case counterpart, because resilience will be priced and discounted for by enterprises and governments alike. We discuss what such a structural change will imply for the International Business of international value chains. Nothing comes easy and so the lessons learned were also after the sacrifice of individuals who are rightly termed as "Warriors" who through their sacrifice taught life's greatest lessons that money can buy all but not happiness and life. The power of materialism that has blindfolded all was made to realize all that works is love, compassion and humanity. Hence rightly goes the saying *Service to Humanity Is Service to God.*

References

^ Bostock, Bill (13 February 2020). "China sacked a brace of top officials in Hubei province, likely in a move to protect Xi Jinping from people's anger over the coronavirus pandemic". Business Insider. Archived from the original on 18 February 2020. Retrieved 26 February2020.

^ Yu, Sun (9 February 2020). "Coronavirus death toll tops SARS as public backlash grows". Financial Times. Archived from the original on 26 February 2020. Retrieved 26 February2020.

^ "Hong Kong protesters torch planned Wuhan virus quarantine building". CNA. Archived from the original on 6 February 2020. Retrieved 26 February 2020.

^ "Taiwan hits out at China virus travel bans". medicalxpress.com. Archived from the original on 26 February 2020. Retrieved 26 February 2020.

^ Vercoe, Peter. "Australia Walks Back Surplus Promise on Deadly Virus, Wildfires". Bloomberg L.P. Archived from the original on 2 February 2020. Retrieved 14 March 2020.

^ Tiezzi, Shannon (6 February 2020). "China and Cambodia: Love in the Time of Coronavirus". Archived from the original on 6 February 2020. Retrieved 10 February2020.

^ Smith, David (14 March 2020). "'I don't take responsibility': Trump shakes hands and spreads blame over coronavirus".

The Guardian. ISSN 0261-3077. Archived from the original on 14 March 2020. Retrieved 15 March 2020.

^ "Fact Check Friday: Trump's coronavirus response plagued with misstatements". ABC News. Archived from the original on 14 March 2020. Retrieved 15 March 2020.

^ Collinson, Stephen. "Trump address sparks chaos as coronavirus crisis deepens". CNN. Archived from the original on 14 March 2020. Retrieved 15 March 2020.

^ Burns, Katelyn (13 March 2020). "Trump's 7 worst statements on the coronavirus pandemic". Vox. Archived from the original on 14 March 2020. Retrieved 15 March2020.

^ "Trump struggles to explain why he disbanded his global health team". MSNBC.com. Archived from the original on 15 March 2020. Retrieved 15 March 2020.

^ Cunningham, Erin; Bennett, Dalton. "Coronavirus pummels Iran leadership as data show spread is far worse than reported". Washington Post. Archived from the original on 14 March 2020. Retrieved 15 March 2020.

^ "Iran Says 10 Percent of Iranian Lawmakers Infected With Coronavirus". National Review. 3 March 2020. Archived from the original on 13 March 2020. Retrieved 15 March2020.

^ Agencies. "Iran: 124 dead from virus including FM's adviser, could use force to stop travel". www.timesofisrael.com. Archived from the original on 18 March 2020. Retrieved 15 March 2020.

^ "Will Iran's Regime Survive Coronavirus?". National Review. 12 March 2020. Archived from the original on 14 March 2020. Retrieved 15 March 2020.

^ Interview with La7 TV aired on 10 March 2020

^ ""ECR Risk Experts Contemplate another Financial Crisis", Euromoney, March 20 2020 - Jeremy Weltman".

^ "Iran bans printing of all newspapers, citing spread of coronavirus". cpj.org.

^ Mustasilta, Katariina (2020). "FROM BAD TO WORSE?: The impact(s) of Covid-19 on conflict dynamics". Conflict Series. European Union Institute for Security Studies (EUISS). Retrieved 1 August 2020.

^ "Transcript of the Secretary-General's virtual press encounter on the appeal for global ceasefire". United Nations Secretary-General. 23 March 2020. Retrieved 1 August 2020.

^ "COVID-19: UN chief calls for global ceasefire to focus on 'the true fight of our lives'". UN News. 23 March 2020. Retrieved 1 August 2020.

^ "170 signatories endorse UN ceasefire appeal during COVID crisis". UN News. 24 June 2020. Retrieved 1 August 2020.

^ "S/RES/2532(2020) - E - S/RES/2532(2020)". undocs.org. Retrieved 1 August 2020.

^ "COVID-19 Educational Disruption and Response". UNESCO. 4 March 2020. Retrieved 29 March 2020.

^ Fisher, Max; Bubola, Emma (15 March 2020). "As Coronavirus Deepens Inequality, Inequality Worsens Its Spread". The New York Times. Retrieved 2 April 2020.

^ Buchanan, Larry; Patel, Jugal K.; Rosenthal, Brian M.; Singhvi, Anjali (1 April 2020). "A Month of Coronavirus in New York City: See the Hardest-Hit Areas". The New York Times. Retrieved 2 April 2020.

^ Madrid, Stephen Burgen Sam Jones in (1 April 2020). "Poor and vulnerable hardest hit by pandemic in Spain". The Guardian. Retrieved 1 April 2020.

^ "Coronavirus May Disproportionately Hurt the Poor—And That's Bad for Everyone". Time. Retrieved 2 April 2020.

^ "Coronavirus: 5.4m Americans lost health insurance during pandemic, report says". The Independent. 15 July 2020.

^ "27 million Americans could lose health insurance as Congress proposes industry 'bailout'". The Independent. 13 May 2020.

^ "Up to 43m Americans could lose health insurance amid pandemic, report says". The Guardian. 20 May 2020.

^ Thompson, Derek (20 March 2020). "The Coronavirus Will Be a Catastrophe for the Poor". The Atlantic. Retrieved 2 April 2020.

^ Burke, Daniel (14 March 2020). "What churches, mosques and temples are doing to fight the spread of coronavirus". CNN. Archived from the original on 14 March 2020. Retrieved 16 March 2020.

^ Parke, Caleb (13 March 2020). "Churches cancel Sunday service, move online amid coronavirus pandemic". Fox News. Archived from the original on 15 March 2020. Retrieved 16 March 2020.

^ "Coronavirus Disease 2019 (COVID-19)". Evangelical Lutheran Church in America. 2019. Archived from the original on 18 March 2020. Retrieved 17 March 2020.

^ Sheva, Arutz (15 February 2020). "Thousands to pray at Western Wall for end to COVID-19 epidemic". Israel National News. Archived from the original on 18 March 2020. Retrieved 17 March 2020.

^ Solovy, Alden (27 February 2020). "Coronavirus: A Prayer for Medical Scientists". Union for Reform Judaism. Archived from the original on 18 March 2020. Retrieved 17 March2020.

^ Trump, Donald (14 March 2020). "Proclamation on the National Day of Prayer for all Americans Affected by the Coronavirus Pandemic and for our National Response Efforts". The White House. Archived from the original on 17 March 2020. Retrieved 17 March2020.

^ Casiano, Louis (13 March 2020). "Trump declares Sunday a National Day of Prayer amid coronavirus crisis". Fox News. Archived from the original on 18 March 2020. Retrieved 17 March 2020.

^ Parke, Caleb (16 March 2020). "Trump, millions go to church online on National Day of Prayer amid coronavirus". Fox News. Archived from the original on 17 March 2020. Retrieved 17 March 2020.

^ "Mental health and psychosocial considerations during the COVID-19 outbreak" (PDF). World Health Organization. 18 March 2020.

^ "Coronavirus Disease 2019 (COVID-19): If You Have Animals". cdc.gov. 11 February 2020.

^ الحيواناتالأليفةلاتنقلفيروسكورونا. فنانونعربفيرسالةلمتابعيهم arabic.cnn.com (in Arabic). 31 March 2020.

^ "UK coronavirus lockdown: the new rules, and what they mean for daily life". Telegraph. 3 April 2020.

^ Gunnell, David; et al. (21 April 2020). "Suicide risk and prevention during the COVID-19 pandemic". The Lancet. Retrieved 27 April 2020.

^ Baker, Noel (22 April 2020). "Warning Covid-19 could lead to spike in suicide rates". Irish Examiner. Retrieved 27 April 2020.

^ "The Guardian view on Brazil and the Amazon: don't look away | Editorial". The Guardian. 5 June 2020. Retrieved 9 June 2020.

^ Hassan, Jennifer. "During quarantine, balconies worldwide set the stage for DJ sets, squats and singing". Washington Post. Retrieved 29 March 2020.

^ Ryan, Shannon.

2. Wright[AQ1], M.O.D. & A.S. Masten. 2005. Resilience processes in development: fostering positive adaptation in the context of adversity. In Handbook of Resilience in Children.

S. Goldstein & R. Brooks, Eds.: 17–37. Kluwer Academic/Plenum. New York.

3. Masten, A.S. 1989. Resilience in development: implications of the study of successful adaptation for developmental psychopathology. In The Emergence of a Discipline: Rochester Symposium on Developmental Psychopathology. D. Cicchetti, Ed.: 261–294.Vol 1. Lawrence Erlbaum Associates. Hillsdale, NJ.

4. Masten, A.S. & J.D. Coatsworth. 1998. The development of competence in favorable and unfavorable environments: lessons from research on successful children. Am. Psychol. 53: 205–220. 5. Cicchetti, D. & W.J. Curtis. 2006. The developing brain and neural plasticity: implications for normality, psychopathology, and resilience. In Developmental Masten & Obradovic: Competence and Resilience in Development 25 Psychopathology: Developmental Neuroscience. D. Cicchetti & D.J. Cohen, Eds.: 1–64. Vol 2. Second edition. Wiley. Hoboken, NJ. 6. Masten, A.S. 2006. Developmental psychopathology: pathways to the future. Int. J. Behav. Dev. 31: 46–53.

7. Masten, A.S. & A.H. Gewirtz. 2006. Vulnerability and resilience in early child development. In: Handbook of Early Childhood Development. K. McCartney & D.A. Phillips, Eds.: Blackwell. 22–43. Malden, MA. 8. Luthar, S.S. 2006. Resilience in development: a synthesis of research across five decades. In Developmental Psychopathology: Risk, Disorder, and Adaptation. D. Cicchetti & D.J. Cohen, Eds.: Vol 3. Second edition. Wiley. New York.

9. Masten, A.S., K. Burt& J.D. Coatsworth. 2006. Competence and psychopathology in development. In Developmental Psychopathology. D. Ciccheti & D. Cohen, Eds.: Second edition. Wiley. New York.

10. Weissberg, R.P., K.L. Kumpfer & M.E.P. Seligman. 2003. Prevention that works for children and youth: an introduction. Am. Psychol. 58: 425–432.

11. Patterson, J. 2002. Understanding family resilience. J. Clin. Psychol. 58: 233– 246. 12. Doll, B., S. Zucker & K. Brehm. 2006. Resilient Classroom: Creating Health Environments for Learning. Guilford. New York.

13. Wang, M.C. & E.W. Gordon. 1994. Educational Resilience in Inner-City America: Challenges and Prospects. Lawrence Erlbaum Associates. Hillsdale, NJ.

14. Murphy, L.B. 1962. The Widening World of Childhood: Paths Toward Mastery. Basic Books. New York.

15. Masten, A.S. & J.L. Powell. 2003. A resilience framework for research, policy, and practice. In Resilience and Vulnerability: Adaptation in the Context of Childhood Adversities. S.S. Luthar, Ed.: 1–25. Cambridge University Press. New York.

16. Roisman, G.I., A.S. Masten, J.D. Coatsworth & A. Tellegen. 2004. Salient and emerging developmental tasks in the transition to adulthood. Child Dev. 75: 1–11.

17. Masten, A.S. & M-G.J. Reed. 2002. Resilience in development. In Handbook of Positive Psychology. C.R.

Snyder & S.J. Lopez, Eds.: 74–88. Oxford University Press. London.

18. Masten, A.S. 2001. Ordinary magic: resilience processes in development. Am. Psychol. 56: 227–238.

19. Masten, A.S., J.D. Coatsworth, J. Neemann, et al. 1995. The structure and coherence of competence from childhood through adolescence. Child Dev. 66: 1635–1659.

20. Masten, A.S., G. Roisman, J.D. Long, et al. 2005. Developmental cascades: linking academic achievement, externalizing and internalizing symptoms over 20 years. Dev. Psychol. 41: 733–746. 21. Gottlieb, G. 1998. The significance of biology for human development: a developmental psychobiological systems view. In Handbook of Child Psychology. W. Damon & R.M. Lerner, Eds.: 233–273.Vol 1. Fifth edition. John Wiley & Sons. New York. 22. Masten, A.S., A. Shaffer. 2006. How families matter in child development: reflections from research on risk and resilience. In Families Count: Effects on Child and Adolescent Development. A. C-S & J. Dunn, Eds.: 5–25. Cambridge University Press. Cambridge. 26 Annals New York ACA

About the Authors

Dr. Swayam Prabha Satpathy has several years of teaching experience in various capacities. Presently, she is working as the Professor in Communication in the Department of Humanities "Siksha O Anusandhan University". She has been awarded with Siksha Ratan Puraskar, Teacher's Excellence award and Best Academician Award, Special Award from Indian Institution of Industrial Engineering. She has also attended, presented papers, given keynote address and chaired sessions in many National and International Conferences such as National University of Singapore 2013, Imperial College of London 2016 and Harvard Cambridge University, Boston, USA 2019. She is associated and is the state editorial head of Shankaracharya Swami Nischalananda Saraswati congregation Puri, Odisha. She is a life member of "Journal of Contemporary Thought" and is the Section Head Editor (Language and Linguistics) of Rupkatha Journal on Interdisciplinary Studies in Humanities. She has also been a resource person for several universities and has conducted Faculty Development Programme in various universities. She is the Founding Chairperson for Swayam Prabha Foundation.

Mr. Akarshak Bose – An enterprising student who is an entrepreneur at heart and writer by passion. He has published first edition of his debut books titled as "An odyssey in perpetual Corridors" and "Inspite of her Thousand Mistakes". He is associated with numerous Start Up companies such as Edustack, Karukarya, Decolane and Tmega which works towards Education and Development. Presently, he is a student at SRM Institute of Science and Technology Ramapuram. He has been awarded with Best Manager Award by REST Society for Research International. He is also Executive Chairman of Jarnsdel Bharathi Foundation and co-chairs Swayam Prabha Foundation. Akarshak is also a good orator and a widely traveled person who delivered numerous talks across India.

www.ingramcontent.com/pod-product-compliance
Lightning Source LLC
LaVergne TN
LVHW100406181026
850499LV00037B/623
* 9 7 8 9 3 5 4 4 6 0 1 8 0 *